TRUE TRANS BIKE REBEL

TAKING

THE LANE

#15

tRue tRaNs BiKe ReBeL

Edited by Lydia Rogue
with Elly Blue

TakingTheLane.com
Portland, ORE

TAKING THE LANE #15
TRUE TRANS BIKE REBEL

edited by Lydia Rogue with Elly Blue, 2019
This Edition © Microcosm Publishing, 2019
All work remains property of its creator © 2018
First Printing

Elly Blue Publishing, an imprint of
Microcosm Publishing
2752 N Williams Ave.
Portland, OR 97227
(503) 799-2698
TakingTheLane.com
Find more feminist bicycle books, zines,
and art at www.microcosm.Pub

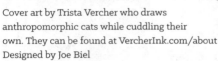

Cover art by Trista Vercher who draws
anthropomorphic cats while cuddling their
own. They can be found at VercherInk.com/about
Designed by Joe Biel

ISBN 978-1-62106-001-7
This is Microcosm #347

Get in touch with your submissions for the next issue of *Taking the Lane*!
Please send submissions and inquiries to elly@microcosmpublishing.com or
learn more about the zine at TakingTheLane.com

Library of Congress Cataloging-in-Publication Data
Names: Rogue, Lydia, editor.
Title: True trans bike rebel / edited by Lydia Rogue.
Description: Portland, OR : Elly Blue Publishing, [2018] | Series: Taking
the
    lane ; #15 | Includes bibliographical references.
Identifiers: LCCN 2018039032 | ISBN 9781621060017 (pbk.)
Subjects: LCSH: Cyclists--Biography. | Transgender people--Biography. |
    Cycling--Psychological aspects.
Classification: LCC GV1051.A1 T78 2018 | DDC 796.6/20922 [B] --dc23
LC record available at https://lccn.loc.gov/2018039032

Microcosm Publishing is Portland's most diversified publishing house and distributor with a focus on the colorful, authentic, and empowering. Our books and zines have put your power in your hands since 1996, equipping readers to make positive changes in their lives and in the world around them. Microcosm emphasizes skill-building, showing hidden histories, and fostering creativity through challenging conventional publishing wisdom with books and bookettes about DIY skills, food, bicycling, gender, self-care, and social justice. What was once a distro and record label was started by Joe Biel in his bedroom and has become among the oldest independent publishing houses in Portland, OR. We are a politically moderate, centrist publisher in a world that has inched to the right for the past 80 years. More recently, Elly Blue Publishing/Taking the Lane merged with Microcosm Publishing in 2015.

Since 2010, Taking The Lane is a feminist bicycle zine. Find past issues and contribute to future ones at

TAKINGTHELANE.COM

TABLE OF CONTENTS

INTRODUCTION

Lydia Rogue

Here's a confession: I'm not much of a cyclist.

I *own* a bike, and take it out for a ride now and again, but it's not really "my thing." Instead, I swim.

And there's an eloquent metaphor I could paint. It would draw parallels between swimming and cycling, and it would conclude that they're part of the same general community, even though they're different—the same way all trans and nonbinary people have their own experiences and move through life in their own way but still connect through the same community.

There are metaphors everywhere for cycling and being trans.

I could make one about the time I flew over the handlebars of my bike when I was twelve, shredding palms and knees on gravel and compare it to the pain of being misgendered or the pain of being trans/nonbinary in a cis-centric world.

There's yet another, pointing out the similarities between getting back on my bike for the first time, almost a year later, and coming out for the first time, or between the spike of fear you get when a car comes just a little too close and the dreaded moment when you get clocked as trans.

There's a less painful, equally eloquent metaphor I could make, comparing the freedom of riding a bike, pushing yourself a little further and soaking in the adrenalin, to gender euphoria.

There are more metaphors, good and bad, than there are spokes in a bike shop, so I'm not going to elaborate on them here. You know them all already, you've likely made them yourself at some point in your life. (We all know that the only way to deal with the pain sometimes is to make a joke at your own expense.)

This isn't a place for metaphors or for distilling our experiences down into small pieces that cis people can swallow—that cis people can understand.

This is a place for *us*.

This is a place where we can simply be, without prying eyes making demands on how we present or invading our spaces demanding we do emotional labor for them. This is a place that has been carved out with us in mind. If you like, it's a safe space where we can talk and laugh and share our experiences and learn that it's okay if we don't fit into the stereotypes—and it's okay if we do.

But where is this place?

Taking the Lane #1 was called *Sharing the Road with Boys*. It focused on Elly Blue's encounters on a sexist road and having to deal with the day-to-day misogyny found in riding while being a cis woman.

To me, *Taking the Lane* means women taking what women deserve—taking a part of the world that had been denied to them for so long, being *allowed* to take up space—to be loud, to be angry, to be heard.

With everything going on in the world, and specifically the US, it's impossible to claim that cis women have finally been granted this freedom, but at the same time, it's easy to see how cis women are granted privileges and rights that trans and nonbinary people can only dream of.

Because of this, for this issue we're taking up the space we deserve too.

I've said this before, and I'll say it again: this issue is about us, by us, for us. We get to be wholly ourselves in this issue without trying to force ourselves into boxes that have to be checked off before we can be given basic treatments.

There are no boxes here, only open roads and open spaces for everyone to be themselves. This is our lane, and so I hope you enjoy it as much as I have.

On a more serious note, please use discretion when reading through the zine. Our lives are not gentle ones, free from oppression and difficulties. Within these pages, you'll read stories of transphobia, abuse, homophobia, sexual assault and more. Sadly, this is part of our current day to day lives, an inescapable reality of living in a ciscentric world. Every story will be preceded by appropriate content warnings, so please heed them and use self-care as needed while reading these stories. To leave out these things would be dishonest about how we move through this world and so they're present.

Love,

Lydia

they/them

EVERYTHING I NEEDED TO KNOW ABOUT BEING TRANS I LEARNED ON THE PAN-AMERICAN HIGHWAY

Elly Bangs

cw: suicidal ideation

On Exhaustion

There were days of squeaking pitifully through the middle of a thousand miles of desert with a gritty headwind whipping me in the face against every turn of the crank—just like there are days when I get misgendered one or ten or a hundred times too many. There were afternoons spent hauling myself straight up the Sierra Madre in a sweltering heat, and evenings when I was too exhausted to reach the next town, or to even pitch a tent where I stealth camped—and all night long, wild dogs came down from the hills to sniff my face and scatter my half-dreams.

A year later those days became the perfect metaphor for the ones when transition felt impossible; when I exceeded my pain tolerance; when I couldn't make myself believe my skin could ever be more than an ill-fitting disguise or a utilitarian means to some end. For an inward eternity, I was climbing a ten thousand foot hill and looking up into the clouds, then rising to meet them, then breathing them in and shivering through their mist, then looking down on them from above, watching them crawl and churn against a cliffside that could've been perched on the edge of outer space. One day on the road I looked back and tried to mentally calculate the angle from where I was to where I'd started, and it dawned on me that to do that now I'd have to look down and through the mantle of the Earth; many times in transition I despaired to think nothing had really changed, until I stumbled on some old photo—and in its sheer strangeness, in the disbelief that I had ever been that person, I re-realized that everything had. I never thought of myself as someone with the will or endurance to make it nearly so far—but I exerted just a little bit every day until it added up to something amazing. To someone I never knew I had it in myself to be.

• • •

A year before I came out, I rode a bicycle alone from Seattle to Panama. Those six months and six thousand miles were many different things to me, and there's no one single narrative I could hang on them that would do justice to what they meant at the time, or what they came to mean in hindsight. The best I can do is this: it was a kind of death wish, but it also saved my life, because it taught me things I needed to know.

On Leaving

People tend to ask what inspired me to do it—quit my job, dump my girlfriend, vacate my apartment, box up or give away everything I owned, and leave my entire life behind to roll away down the highway shoulder with no specific destination and no particular plan to ever return—and I always struggle to answer. It's awkward to mention in casual conversation that at the time I left, I had been mired in self-harm and suicidal ideation for approximately half my life. I had everything I thought I could legitimately need to be happy and I couldn't imagine living past my thirtieth birthday.

Between my own experiences and what others have shared with me, I've come to suspect that there's a distinct quality to the suicidality closeted trans people sometimes deal with: a screaming tension drawn between the basic unbearability of life as it is and the overwhelming certainty that it *could be* something beautiful and valuable in and of itself. I couldn't live, and I couldn't simply die. When I got out of school in 2007 and found myself staring into the abyss of adulthood trying to be a man, I made a deal with myself: I'd spend the next four years trying to build a life worth living, but I'd also be saving up—because if Plan A failed, my Plan B was to leave it all behind and wander the far reaches of the Earth indefinitely.

When it became clear that I'd be resorting to the latter, I knew bicycle touring was the perfect way to do it: it made my body into a means to an end, a machine I could keep in working order and appreciate for its cold, mechanical efficiency. It spared me from the horror of having to treat the body as an end unto itself.

Leaving was one of the hardest things I'd ever done. Even if nothing I had in Seattle amounted to a life I could stand, some of it was beautiful, and all of it was familiar and known. I looked down the road south and only knew I couldn't know what I'd find there.

By the time I stopped pretending to be a man a year later, I was very skilled at pretending. I knew what people expected of me and I knew how to perform it for them without showing the strain or the scars. It was hell, but it was my hell, and I knew how it all worked. I knew the same couldn't be said for the ways of being I was moving into.

Nothing makes leaving easy, even if it's necessary. Even when you know staying might kill you.

On Fear

A lot of strangers, mostly white men RV-camping in state parks, tried to put the fear of crossing in me on my way down the U.S. Pacific coast. The closer I came to the border the more I dreaded to admit to anyone that I was planning to cross it. I came to understand that in the collective mind of white America, traveling to any part of Mexico outside the tourist bubbles is tantamount to falling out the bottom of the world. By the time I reached Tijuana, I had to shush the voice they'd installed in the back of my head to warn me that I'd surely be skinned alive by narco-terrorists the moment I crossed. *It's another planet,* they seemed to say. *An alien planet. A hostile world where people like you and I can never belong, can never be safe.*

A lot of people tried to put the fear of transition in me too: I mean all the cisgender people across all of time who've built the commonplace understanding of trans people up into a spectacle of ugliness, tragedy, rejection, danger. I mean all the men I ever knew who spoke of women as if they inhabited an insurmountably bizarre and alien world; who spoke of the border between genders as binary, ironclad, razor-sharp, impossible to cross, and anyone who so much as tried was surely doomed. So many people put so much fear in me that by the time I approached that crossing I believed I'd be disowned by everyone I knew. I thought transition meant falling out the bottom of the world.

All I found in Mexico was the cruel absurdity of borders. I saw the towering walls fear-stricken white Americans had already erected, complete with razor wire and prison yard towers and swarms of black helicopters. I met the families that wall has sawed in half and the people who travel across it continually, and everything on the far side was different and yet no part of it was alien. I discovered that, in spite of the relentless and fevered machinations of people who live in terror of borders that can be crossed, this continent is one place, one continuous humanity. The same is true of gender.

This is not to say there is no danger in crossing. I know well that my privileges as a middle-class white person protected me on the other side of that wall, and they protect me now on the other side of transition. I met many Mexicans who themselves didn't feel safe in Mexico and I can only dream of a world in which trans people, especially trans people of color, feel safe being trans, or where women in general feel safe being women. But there's a difference between the fears you gain from experience and live with by necessity, and the fears other people, never really knowing, will try to put in you to keep you on your assigned side.

On Being Weird

Wherever I went, I was weird. The farther south I traveled the more truly bizarre I became to everyone. The road took me through towns where I was the palest person in sight—and I was a six-foot-two-inch-tall giant, clad in frayed spandex, squeaking along in the highway shoulder with sixty pounds of baggage hanging off my frame and an unkempt bright red beard growing past my collarbone. In some places people stood on the roadside and stared, wordless, unmoving, open-mouthed, for however long it took me to pass by. It depressed me terribly.

The day I crossed into Guatemala I started climbing a hill that turned out to be ten thousand feet tall at a consistent six to ten percent grade. By the end of that day I was encrusted in my own salt and my emotional reserves were more than spent. When a bus pulled up ahead of me and let ten children out onto the shoulder, I felt a great wave of despair: These kids were going to stare at me, I thought. They were going to gawk long and hard, and I was going to be stuck there in their line of sight for five or ten minutes while I crawled past them in my granny gear. And sure enough, they stared—but as I got close they all smiled and started cheering me on: *¡Ánimo! ¡Ánimo! ¡Ánimo!*[1] To this day I consider this the happiest single moment of my life.

Somewhere on that highway, I made my peace with the risk of seeming weird to people. There will always be someone to gawk at my height or the sound of my voice or whatever else they'll use to consign me to some liminal space in their minds. But the things that make me different are my mountain to climb, and I'm proud of every grueling switchback I've hauled myself up. I take pride in my weirdness. Every once in a while, I find someone else who does too.

On Getting Lost in the Night

There were long days. Some turned into nights. Sometimes the sun set on me before I could find anywhere to rent a bunk or pitch a tent—and when there was no light by which to read my cycle computer, I rolled on with no way of knowing how far I'd gone or how long I'd been pedaling; the road in my headlight stretched out into deep space and infinite time. After minutes that could've been hours,

1 This directly translates to 'spirit'; my sense is that its closest approximation in English would be 'eyes on the prize!'

I started to wonder if I'd missed my turn to the next town. After hours that could've been days I began to wonder if there *was* any next town. Maybe I was dead, and this was a purgatory commensurate with my deeds in life: riding this bicycle alone through a night with no end, no street lamps, no signposts, no other traffic, nothing but the stars above the void of the treeline. There was no way to navigate. No way to know.

When I was a child I imagined that growing up would be a process of learning more and more about the world, until I understood it fully. I imagined that being an adult meant knowing what to do: Always having a map and always knowing how to read it. I spent the years before my transition roiling in self-doubt; I told myself I couldn't be trans because I'd never felt a sufficiently crystalline certainty about who or what I was. But I truly started growing up the day I realized that there were no maps for the places I needed to go, and no light by which to read them—when I stopped searching for some external rubric to tell me whether or not I was trans enough—when I figured out that the defining virtue of maturity is not certainty, but the ability to operate elegantly in the total absence of certainty.

Every time I got lost in the night I learned to be more at home on those lightless backroads. Somewhere out there I learned the art of not knowing. Then the glittering city lights would break like a dawn just over the last hill or around the last bend, and I'd fill my stomach with street food and sing for joy that my faith in the other side of the night had been vindicated. Two years later I'd recognize how my skin had changed and feel much the same thing.

On Arrival

To reach Panama City, I had to cross the Bridge of the Americas, a towering high-speed behemoth arching over the mouth of the Canal. I was terrified to ride across it until I saw my perfect stroke of luck: A taxi had stalled right at the top of the bridge, leaving the whole right lane clear of traffic. I took my time climbing. I watched the freight ships passing way beneath my pedals and stared out across the Pacific in the day's last light. The sky was a deep purple, the hills all vivid green, and as I rose toward the apex I looked ahead and saw the narrow, mirrored skyscrapers of Panama City stabbing up between them, clad in the burning light of the sunset. Downtown looked like a golden Oz, too absurdly beautiful to be real. I must have laughed the whole way down the other side.

That wasn't quite the end of my trip, but it was one of many moments of arrival. I was exactly where I needed to be then: I was at home in the world. There's no final end to a transition either—what animal ever stops changing?— but I've found there are moments of arrival there too: In the first time I was able to see myself as myself; in the first time I knew someone else did; in any given day now when I manage to take a breath and stop to realize that I made it. I survived. I evolved. And I am finally, finally finding a home in myself.

NICEPEOPLE

Jace

cw: misogyny, misgendering, suicidal ideation

my first job at a shop, i am hired during the first interview. when i quit that job two years later, boss-man laments how hard it is to hire women.

a customer asks if i am for sale, or if i am included with the bicycle, like a shot of jack with the purchase of the kind of beer that reminds me of when i was as young as i look. he was not asked to leave.

i ride my bicycle seventeen miles each way to emerson hospital for my pre- and post-op appointments. i lock my bike to the railing next to where the valet attendant stands. he laughs. i have to explain i am there alone, but also i don't need to validate my parking. i ride my bicycle an hour early to my ultrasound at beth israel so i will have time to sit outside and drink 32 oz of water. i lock up on the employee rack.

the first time i ride after top surgery is ten days after, weeks before the doctor said to. i am hit from behind by another cyclist, eat shit in the middle of mass ave and vassar. when people chastise me for not wearing a helmet, i tell them if i get hit by a car i better die.

a cop pulls up next to me after i made an illegal right turn. she rolls down the window, not even stopping and yells, hey kid, next time you have to wait for the light, okay? i am white.

the nurse watching as a give myself my first t shot notices my grimy hands, asks if i'm a mechanic. good for you, she says, there aren't very many women in that industry.

i stab myself.

you know what i mean, she says.

someone i knew in high school interviews to live in my house. we interact as strangers. during the tour she says wow you have bike parking. no that's just my room. i never tell her i know her. she does not move into my house.

i shave my face every day before i host the wtf repair night. i've stopped giving my pronouns. the facilitator has started to make an explicit point of saying trans mascs are welcome.

i put on my scruff profile ftm4nicepeople (or people to mtb with me). someone messages me to ask what mtb[2] means. i thought it was a queer thing, he says.

my instagram profile reads: pansy transsexual bike mechanic. i put up pictures of my bikes in wooded locations. most of my followers post pictures of their greyhounds.

---

2 mountain biking

BUILD YOUR OWN BODY

Laurie Williams

I build this bike with my own hands. I picture myself on it—the adventures I will have and the distance I will go. I choose the handlebar tape to match the saddle. Component by component, I make it, fit it together. If something doesn't feel right, I listen, I examine and I diagnose. Add a few extra spacers here and there on the headset. Saw a few millimetres off the chain ring for better clearance. Hold things together with protective electrical tape until I can think of a neater solution.

As I design its blueprint in my mind, I start to design myself in the same way. Subconsciously at first, in daydreams and just before sleep. Slowly, these plans start to unfurl; steadily transforming from abstraction into something tangible. What geometry do I want for myself? How will I form these new shapes? What tools do I need? A sketch is drawn, a path to follow until I get there.

He sits opposite me and looks me wearily in the eye, just waiting to tick his boxes. I know what he expects from me, so I give it to him. Yes, I'm uncomfortable. Yes, this body is holding me back. He nods sympathetically, scribbling my life story in shorthand. I'm one of many appointments today, and that number gets larger every day. He just needs to hear me hit a few key notes. It's easier to follow a flow chart than to start from scratch with every new person who walks through your door. It's easier to build a bike you'll never be expected to ride.

Afterwards I take a deep breath and thank him, shake his hand whilst he wishes me luck. I pick up my helmet and walk out the door, gripping the envelope containing my prescription. As I ride away, the lactic acid builds in my calves to an angry crescendo. I need to feel their pathology evaporate off my skin with the sweat that cools me. I apologize to myself, to my body, which has never held me back. But there isn't a box for that kind of self-determination. As I put the miles between now and what went before, I steer myself towards something greater.

As I ride, the feeling floods back and I return to who I am. When I'm on my bike, I'm free of their bureaucracy. I'm a flash of ambiguous Cinelli blue to the pedestrians I fly by on the pavement, passing them too quickly for their brains to scramble my body into a category. My bike is my accomplice, my getaway vehicle as I speed away from the gatekeeping; the mix up on the system; the misspelling on the envelope. Every downward push of the pedal channels my rage from my chest through my legs and safely into the tarmac. And so it goes on. I adapt my body like I do my bike. It isn't textbook and it works perfectly.

MOVEMENT

Sybil Collas

cw: injury, blood

I had never broken a single bone until I rode a skateboard. It wasn't my idea: my companion was just dead set on riding something and, being the love-struck idiot that I am, I jumped on the first website I could find to search for wheeled things.

We chose the smallest models, two mini Penny boards, because the bigger ones looked too easy and we were not the kind to refuse a challenge. We were thinking like children. Falling when you're a kid is alright, you're close to the floor, there's not much space to develop a real impact. However, as an adult, your weight is much more developed, and your height makes for a drop of two to four interminable seconds. I'd say my fall took an average three seconds—the chin bouncing on concrete taking most of that time before I could stabilize into a steady position. I saw a little mountain right before my eyes, all nice and shiny, and realized my teeth actually looked pretty good. When I licked my dentition to check for gaps, I felt the warmth of blood—which was so cliché, iron taste and everything—and tiny bits of ivory scratched against my tongue. Later, I recited my French social security number and displayed that displeased look you have when you try to mumble through a torn mouth and the first numeral of your most important identification number outs your genitals to everyone in the emergency service. One is a penis. Two is a vagina. Fucking skateboard.

We bought bigger boards: a longboard for him, a brake-system model for me. In a fit of salary-induced frenzy, we left for a weekend in Barcelona. The sun gave me the lobster tan of red-hair people and forced me to wear clothes that highlighted my shapes. Thanks to the heat, the streets were dry and silky—we fought against the bumpy pavement for a little while before the road became smooth under us, and we glided along the seaside and into the night. The salty breeze stung my burn marks and the scar on my chin. Lighting was sparse, and both streets and people disappeared in shadows; we rode to the lights and watched teenagers as they floated together in the insides of a skatepark, unattained by gravity. A guy said my board looked cool. Another called out to me to know where I'd gotten it. I couldn't remember, I was too focused on what he had called me. 'Hey, man.' It felt incredible.

My social security number still doesn't accept 0 as a valid option. The skateboard was sold, and I retreated to the safety of a kick scooter, which makes me look nicer than a bike does when I wear a skirt. Sometimes I walk. Sometimes I don't. When you go too fast for strangers to take your silhouette in, the vision that remains in them is that of a blurry and undefined person. But in my mind, the image is always clear. I'm not a rider or a walker, not really. I'm the movement in between.

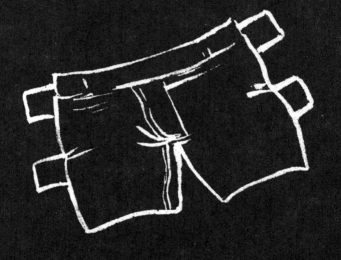

WHEN EVEN YOUR UNDERWEAR'S STRESSED

Liz Tetu

My legs kick ass. Particularly my own.

Pulling a coarse-right, then glossy-left, boot heel against my butt, tentatively pretending to perform ballistic stretches off the recycled park benches tucked into the swamp trail, eating bugs, sometimes I forget that it wasn't the low lung capacity I ended up calculating for some high school gym class that had kept me walking the emerald paths behind the trailer park. I don't even think about it as I reach up into the gaping legs of my shorts and adjust my boxers during those breathers.

Many of the funny folks I know aren't ready to humor me for accomplishing an hour's amble, although I get a one-liner or two about having kept it up almost every day for the last six months. I love my friends, but I know it's up to me to remember that I used to barely manage sparse fifteen-minute strolls, that I'm walking now because I'm living trans. My fitness is improving because I'm trans and I care about myself.

Boxers, man.

The social transition from tomboy to young guy was simple, all things considered. The short brittle hair, sarcastic slogans on cotton T-shirts, and faded blue jeans basically did the same thing for strangers as they always did. I went from a heavyset boy to a husky adult with a hefty chest--there wasn't a teaspoon worth of surprise at my changing body to stir into easy-as-pie teen spite. Even explaining that my not-so-new masculine name was Liz to allies, acquaintances, and acolytes was a walk in the park, although that turn of phrase meant diddly nothing to me. There was still something in the way between me and my masculinity.

Enter the panties.

Stuffed into the darkness of my drawers, they were barely a piece of cloth, each awash in lavish dyes that indulged in the polychromatic palette of dull pink, off-white, and cigarette stain yellow. The pairs I kept amounted in the double digits, but the last batch outlasted both the needs of my body and my patience from the age of ten to fifteen years old.

In some ways, it wasn't their snapping elastic that made me nervous. If they worked as underthings, why did I also have to wear bicycle shorts under skirts and dresses? When kid me stumbled into high school anime clubs, across men's and sport's magazines at convenience stores, around the Internet at the public library, where cameras and prosthetic viewers stalked animated girls and fem models and the cotton textile that connected this freaky focus to my clothes and thus my body, light flowy material versus darkness and jean be damned, I was insecure, and terrified.

In some ways, it was these hole-y rags themselves that hurt me. It'd take less than five minutes of walking in them before they'd get twisted around and about half an hour before I started getting a "heat burn," regardless the weather. Without a buffer between my thighs, scalding blood red marks would develop on them, burns no salve could save or powder pamper. (Sometimes I catch the pink and brown scars in the corner of my eye all these years later.) The more cargo shorts and carpenters' pants I wore, air rushing up my legs and making me feel naked when I was supposed to be clothed off, the more noticeable my discomfort was. I lived inside, avoiding physical activity except during my self-destructive moments, trying to push myself past dwindling limits.

It was during one of these sporadic exercises that I stomped towards my first pairs of boxers. The storyteller in me wants to say I marched to the discount retailer the same day my boyfriend pointed out that I didn't have to wear panties if I didn't want to before I literally ripped them off and stuffed the infernal scraps into my backpack. The same day I found out I'd have to take the remaining open gym class, a "women"-focused course, in order to graduate. The same time I first came out as trans in a middle school girl's locker room to a transphobe. Even the time I wore short shorts instead of underwear and loved it. But these kind of happened years apart.

Fifteen with fifteen dollars in my wallet, I walked my ass off, bought the cheapest bag, and scuttled my way home soaked in sweat. I shined. I was a little hoarse.

I mixed them in with the laundry that day. They clung a little tight to my legs and kept me cool and contained. I threw the panties away and donated the bras. I was a man. I discovered my legs. That walk changed my life and I *liked* doing it.

So that's why, panting and dark pink, unfettered by any undershirt and sporting my boxers, my face pops up around town, carried by hirsute limbs and tough boots.

And even though I can say I put my foot against the backside of something detrimental to my wellbeing, an obstacle to my confidence, and pushed, there are some early experiences that I won't get back. I've never ballroom danced in a suit. I've never trick-or-treated and felt comfortable. My masculinity has never been just skin deep, but the greatest hindrance to acting for myself pinched my irritated dermis all those years.

I held onto, stepped into, and strapped on these smallclothes trying to conform in some way to something I can't even rationalize now. Gender norms? Sexual standards? Transphobic and misogynistic arguments? Were panties my *skirt*?

Fortunately, I don't have to go through and try to surface the justifications. I just need to know that today, I'm a content and resilient guy. I walk from grocery store to my partner's house, slathering on sunscreen, to movie theater and park and lake, swimming in trunks and a tank top in the afternoon, and no body stops me.

Outside for five years, I'm still learning more and more about the afternoon joggers in my neighborhood, the ways my calf muscles acquire lactic acid and how my diet alters the process, and just how great the smiles of both overt and quiet queer kids and teens feel when they see themselves surviving in the wild as adult trans and gender nonconforming heroes through me as I visibly trek around the wetland we also share.

I'm also learning how to ride a bike. Finally.

TWO WHEELS, TWO HEARTS

Quinn

Cycle touring was always best alone. It was a break from my constant internal dialogue about whether I should take the plunge and transition. There was no one sirring me on the phone at work. My coworkers weren't there reminding me of how unwelcome I would be if I came out, how I would be the subject of their gossip just like their trans "friends" that they talked about with deadnames and incorrect pronouns. I had room on the road to be kind to myself. Away from it for a second, I was able to be ok with myself, not free from my dysphoria and my feeling of having waited too long to transition, but neutral, not wrong, at least.

Then I was with Allie at Sleeping Bear, confessing my feelings for her by our campfire on our first night out. I played surf pop for us on my phone as we sat back in our fold-up chairs, beat by the riding we'd done, she said it was so gay. She'd inflamed a knee injury, so we were cutting our first tour together short and just staying put, my fault with my lousy distance measurement on the map.

I was so nervous; I wasn't sure that she saw me as someone she could be in a relationship with. She was so understanding of my shyness and insecurities, like she understood why I was the way I was. We both loved riding bikes, too; I'd ride around town on the weekends hoping to run into her. I got her a job at the bike shop I worked at, and when we were alone in back we kissed each other. She said she loved me, too, and we leaned against one another as we cooked bratwurst over the fire and talked about how lucky we were to find each other. We laughed when I chased a raccoon out of our site and up a tree.

Later that night we went and laid together on the beach. The Milky Way snaked overhead. The waves crashed against the beach and the wind was cold off of Lake Michigan. We kissed and snuggled close against each other in our little sand hollow for warmth.

We crawled into bed together late and interlaced our sleeping bags so we could hold our bodies together in spite of our thin, separate mattresses. We smelled like sunscreen, bug spray, and sweat. We fucked in the morning, ignoring the campground host who came around our site on his golf cart. I always liked to start my days as soon as there was any light outside, but we lay together in our tent until it was too hot to stand any longer.

We went into the little town to eat and were nervous together, both of our first times being a gay couple in public. We held hands under the table. Then we climbed to where the dunes overlooked the lake and sat there holding each other's hands.

I wondered whether she was trans and she said that she'd been trying to figure that out. I told her about how I knew I was, but I was so scared I had stopped taking hrt for years, that I wanted to start again but didn't know if I would be strong enough to cope. We stayed for a long time there together. When we left, I felt changed.

Everything was still terrifying, but I felt hopeful in that moment.

TRANS PORTATION

NOTHING DONE

Rufus Isabel Elliot

cw: intense, non-graphic descriptions of sexual assault, violence, gun mention

He gestures at the trees towering beside us—smiles.

We do not share a language, but I assume he is commenting on the beauty and tranquility of nature, the quiet and the sound of the trees on this late summer's day on a deserted road up the mountainside.

And it was beautiful. I was glowing with the cool air and vigorous exercise, the afternoon sun, and the last stream to cross the road for many more hours, flowing with cold mountain water.

Before this man lets me go, he insists on giving me his water bottle, also filled with this same spring water. I know I will drink it, or I will be thirsty before morning.

The road seems all the more deserted now that his car is still. The sounds of birds and of rustling trees are the foreground of our temporary world.

The beauty of this mountain road was not for me. My mistake in even being there was shown to me in no uncertain terms by this man, this man who also thought the forest was beautiful, who also wanted to drink the water, enjoy the sunshine.

This man tried to rape me. He talked about the forest and the road, gave me a cigarette, lit it, asked about my husband, dragged me by the wrists over to his car, and kissed me, laughing, with his hard-on pushing up against my football shorts and the nothingness beneath.

I pushed and fought and bargained, and eventually he decided to let me go, lifted my bike out of his van, gave me one last shove on my way off up the road.

I'll give you this smallish slice of my honour, I said, *if you give me my life.*

I didn't call the police. I didn't phone my zefriend. I didn't run into the forest and hide, in case he changed his mind, and decided to drive up the road after me. I just cycled, up and up, shaking, heart pounding, until hours later I flung myself down on the bare, rocky mountainside.

That shitty mountain road was my only idea—all I wanted was to carry on. Not to protect myself, not to seek justice, or revenge, but to get straight back on my bike and ride on. A one track mind, fuelled by the idea that the road is going to take me somewhere other than my next bivvy spot.

Wherever you are, there is somewhere further you can go.[3] Except sometimes there is nothing and nowhere. There is no way to run, no escape.

Let me make things perfectly clear: I did not escape. He let me go.

There, perched on the mountaintop, I drank the water he gave me, still a little cold, strange on my tongue. By morning I had pissed it away.

---

3 Tim Ingold, *Lines: A Brief History* (London and New York: Routledge, 2016)

My whole body was raw, my hands ached, and my palms felt like tender new skin.

From that pass, I saw in the north a wall of ice spread against the blue of the sky, as though it was floating several kilometres off the surface of the earth. I felt kin with the smallest trickle of melted snow, remembered my icy agenderness, felt a sign had been given that the purity of my own glacier was just as true as it had been two hours before. I texted my zefriend. I saw the way the ice to the north towered jaggedly into the blue, and felt strong and tall.

There was nothing romantic about that mountain journey, nothing romantic about the forest, nothing romantic about the icy horizon that spread out somewhere far beyond me. But I wonder if he thought there was— the way he smiled at me, the way other men have smiled at me, hung around when they should have driven on.

There is nothing to discover in nature; there is no hidden secret.[4]

4 'There is nothing to discover in sex or sexuality; there is no inside.'
Paul B. Preciado, trans. Bruce Benderson, *Testo Junkie: Sex, Drugs, and Biopolitics in the Pharmacopornographic Era* (New York: The Feminist Press, 2016) p.35

There is nothing up there; I have no inside.

What would have happened to me if it had come to it, if he hadn't let me go, if he had then seen the inside was as icy as the outside, deep blue and rotten. My body was totally closed to him: there was nothing there to rape.

I can hardly doubt he would have found a way: I was to be wrested out of the wild and into *nature* by this man, by the bruised lines he made around my arms, and by a hole drilled right through me.

The *wild*—the world of plants and animals—is not cisgender or heterosexual in the obvious biopolitical way, where heterosexuality is coded as 'species typical', where gendered terminology is enforced on critters, where reproductivity and sexual selection are key, and animal relationships are sentimentalised. *Nature*, however, *is* cisgender and heterosexual. It is an anthropocentric space, one that privileges the white cisgender man, gives him power over every other critter he encounters there.

Nature is the tranquility of the forest, the rugged mountain track, something you enjoy on holiday with your girlfriend.

Nature claims to be in some way right, the purity of a world untouched by humanity, but instead it is what is left when the wild is bounded in, forcibly regulated. The *wild* is a space of urgent mutuality, of constantly being-with.[5] You cannot visit it.

Nature is not for ones like me, agender lesbians, boyish critters with no biopenis. That day, in a hinterland between *nature* and the *wild,* I knew I was unwelcome. I was suddenly—violently—out of love with the world.

The *wild* is where I belong, where I am not held by a patriarchal regime that will see what it wants in me: that will dehumanise me in the name of heteronormativity, attempt to rehumanise me in the name of cisnormativity, then decide to have its way with me when it finds me alone *in nature.*

Four days later, another mountain pass, and a young shepherd with dark hair and sad eyes and a sweet, round face is looking at me with accusation. These are his summer pastures, his flock gathered on the hill behind him.

5 See Donna Haraway, *Staying With The Trouble: Making Kin In The Cthulucene* (Durham and London: Duke University Press, 2016)

Only a few hours earlier, in the dead of night, he had crawled up to my body, peeled back its ice blue sleeping bag, and began to touch it: arms, torso, legs. He pushed me back down. He tried to turn me over, making space for himself on the earth beside me, and at long last I choked out—

Please. Stop—

and he crawled away from me, a beast on all fours, passing out on the ground only a few meters away.

In the morning, while I lay there, he lit a fire and heated some bread, literally pushing it into my hands. He put three sugar cubes into a cup of tea for me, and wrapped my cold fingers around it with huge, gentle hands. I wasn't fighting, wasn't saying anything. He poured out some water into a bowl for me to wash with. He watched. And then I was leaving.

The frost of the clear, bright night on that bare mountain pass was slowly fading, and I was crying.

·   ·   ·

Only a few days later, I am tracking north in search of the same snow I saw from the mountaintop a whole lifetime ago. I can no longer stand to follow my compass bearing across the bridge of the world, and so I seek ice.

I cried as another man on another remote road forced his advice on me. He asked me why I never called the police, and I continued to cry.

No more crying, okay?

Don't cry.

Never cry.

He had invited me in for a cup of Nescafe, and a pomegranate from his garden. I had only stopped to read a map, to double check my turnings through his mountain village, but now I am in his flat, and my bike is in his yard. He takes a flick knife out of his pocket to open the fruit—I don't want to show him mine, but I feel its weight against my thigh.

The seeds are like sand in my teeth, my tongue numbed by the acidic taste, like it was numbed by the water another man gave me, only a week before.

He asks me whether I carry a gun. Kalashnikov, yes?

I shrug.

You know Kalashnikov?

He shows me his imaginary weapon.

I shrug again. This is playing with fire.

You are scared, yes?

He doesn't want to let me go, wants to pour me another whisky, proposes a toast, suggests I sleep over. Let's go to Abastumani; let's find this man. I will kill him for you—I will.

He smiles.

But you have to promise not to cry.

I shake my head. Perhaps he thinks he is showing kindness, but I would rather take my chances with the wolves.

No more: I make my camp alone, out in the snow, sleep in all my clothes.

.   .   .

Months pass, and I remain obsessed by these three encounters.

I see the shepherd in the face of the manager at work. I see the man from Abastumani in the face of a stranger waiting at the other side of a crossing, recoil like he's hit me.

And I've imagined the baby I would have had.

Would it have had his magnificently arched nose, his brown skin? Or brown eyes in a foxglove face?

The shepherd's child is easier to picture—a soft face, the widest of smiles.

It would have known all about the kindness of strangers.

But somehow it seems to be a boy either way.

I believed I had healed myself once before. *I liked anything that made me feel strong, that showed me how unbreakable I was.*[6]

I still get in strangers' cars, when I feel strong and whole, making tracks alone in mountain wildernesses.

I didn't find a way, out there on mountain roads day and night. I found dead ends, brutality, loss.

I am not part of the *nature* that enabled these men, made me into a sweet young victim.

My transness crawled out of that solitary wild, and lies beside me every night in my bivvy. It lurks in the layers of grime on my bearskin, and it holds me up on a clear still lake—a kind of ungendered gender euphoria.

My agenderness is unhuman; my body is more glacier than flesh, crags of ice jutting into a distant sky—*all blue*.[7]

---

6 Eileen Myles, *Cool For You: A Novel* (Berkeley: Soft Skull Press, 2000)
7 Ursula Le Guin, *The Left Hand of Darkness* (London: Orbit, 1992)

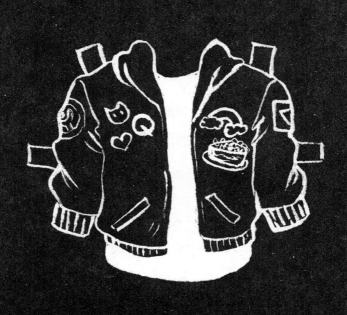

TRUE

TRANS

BIKE

REBEL

Trista Vercher

LATER AT RIVER'S APT...

AAH! DON'T KILL MEE !!!

WUMP WUMP

WHEN I DECIDED TO BUILD A BIKE FROM SCRATCH, IT WASN'T BECAUSE THERE'S ANYTHING WRONG WITH THE ONE I HAVE.

click

IT'S A GOOD BIKE--

FUNCTIONAL.

BUT I DON'T LOVE IT.

I WANT SOMETHING THAT FEELS LIKE IT **BELONGS** TO ME...

SIGH.

--AND THE ONLY WAY I KNOW HOW TO DO THAT IS TO MAKE IT MYSELF, WITH PARTS I CHOOSE AND ASSEMBLE WITH CARE.

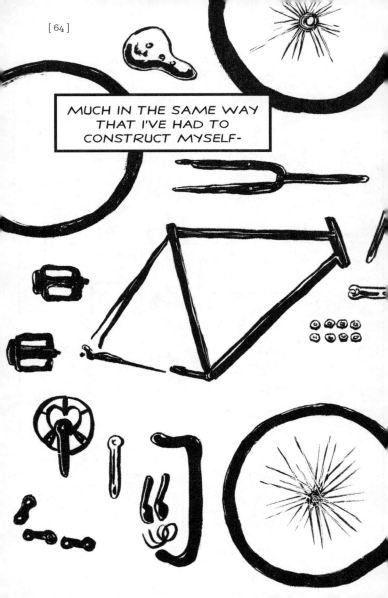

MUCH IN THE SAME WAY
THAT I'VE HAD TO
CONSTRUCT MYSELF-

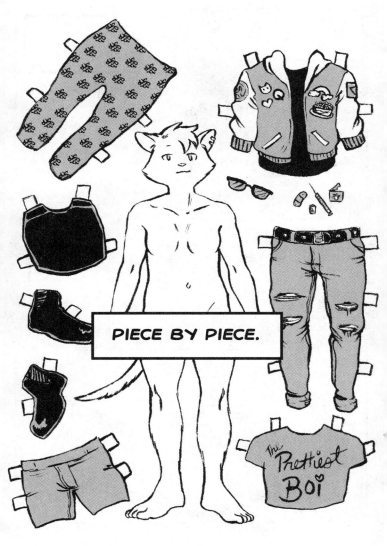

PIECE BY PIECE.

FINDING FEAR, VALIDATION, AND COMMUNITY

Tara Seplavy

cw: gendered slurs, misgendering

On a warm spring day with traffic backed up at a stoplight a couple towns over from where I live, I squeaked my 44-cm-wide bars between the mirrors of a parked car and that of a red Jeep. In the process, my elbow glanced the Jeep's mirror. I thought nothing of it and rode on.

Several hundred yards down the road, the same Jeep drove up close to me. The middle-aged male driver yelled a line of obscenities towards me about never touching his car again. The only word that I really heard was "cunt".

Not since having a handgun pulled on me by a disgruntled driver some twenty years prior had I immediately feared for my life while riding my bike. That one word pierced my thick skin like a bullet and rang through my ears like a gunshot.

There is something about heckling that is universal across cycling in the US. I have had it happen to me, and admittedly I have done it myself on more than one occasion. When done correctly in the context of racing, it can be funny and even elicit a smile from the most stoic of racers. But usually, it seems to be done for purposes of intimidation or for no clear reason at all other than simply to be profane or inane.

In my almost 25-years of racing, I have personally bore witness to some rather classic, and usually tasteless, heckling. From collegiate racing, to cyclocross in New England, to legendary places such as Yardsale at Mount Snow or Hecklers Rock at Whistler, I have pretty much seen or heard it all. Hell, I even saw some of the world's best professional racers being showered with beer and calling cards for sex workers during the infamous Beergate incident during CrossVegas a few years ago.

Growing up and riding in the NYC suburbs you get used to passing cars, homeless guys, or kids playing ball giving you a hard time about being on a bike. It's often comments like "get on the sidewalk" or "hey Lance Armstrong", and usually mixed in with one or more curse words. I'm sure no one would be at all surprised that words hurled at men are often homophobic slurs.).

In my (too) many years presenting as a guy while riding or racing, I struggle to think of a single time where I was actually offended by words thrown my way when on the bike. Be them from spectators on the sides of race tracks or passing drivers in suburbia, the words generally rolled off my shoulders.

I had heard from women riders who were offended by the heckles or derogatory things shouted at them while riding, and even women who gave up racing or switched their solo rides to the indoor trainer to avoid the unwelcome insults. For whatever reason, I never saw it as a serious problem and probably something blown out of proportion on social media. Perhaps testosterone blocks these things from ever really getting into your head, or I was really that pathetically naive.

A lot of things change during transition as you begin to present as your true identity. If you are on HRT, there are often significant physical and emotional changes that shape how others view you, but also how you see the surrounding world. It can be a confusing time and is often filled with a lot of pain as people trip over your name or pronouns or you are misgendered in public. Those little wins when you "pass", when coworkers get your name right in a meeting, or when Mom uses the correct pronouns, can carry you through a day on a good little wave.

On a winter day, about five or six months after I started hormones, and about two months before the run-in with the previously referenced Jeep driver, I ventured outside for a late day road ride. Like a good roadie, I was wearing the matching fluro pink lycra kit of a local women's shop team, a short ponytail peeking out from under my helmet. I didn't think anything of my gender presentation, as it was "just another ride" and I was just happy to be riding outdoors versus on rollers in my basement.

As I was nearing the end of the ride, and only a couple miles from my house, a car pulled up next to me and I heard the words "fucking lesbo" emanate from the open passenger side window. As the car sped away, I chuckled and jokingly yelled back "How did you know?" I was being read as a woman by a driver and he knew I liked women! A tall, big boned, athletic woman must be a lesbian after all, no?

That incident didn't really hit me as being wrong in any way, at first. For weeks I wore it like a badge of honor and shared the story with humorous pride; similar to getting a "yeah girl" yelled at me by another rider on the local mountain bike trail a few weeks prior to that. For the first time in my life, I was being read as a woman on the bike and that felt perfect.

After being called a cunt, it really began to sink in what had happened. I am a woman, and this is how women are treated while riding, as well as in everyday life. This was the reality of my new existence and presentation to the world. I knew there would be a stark contrast between presenting as a woman versus as a man, but validation through misogyny is something I never conceived could exist.

When I began openly and publicly racing as a woman, I honestly expected there to be a lot of blowback and public debate. Being someone entrenched in the bicycle industry, and particularly within the mountain bike world, I expected there to be all sorts of taunts and uproar in the testosterone fueled bicycle social media world. The harassment of trans athletes in cycling (such as Michelle Dumaresq from many years ago) is a large part of what kept me so deep in denial about my own identity.

I was surprised when I started racing that this wasn't really a major problem. Maybe it was because I know folks, or perhaps it was because I am simply not a really good bike racer. I am sure there have been comments, but I guess they must be happening behind my back or on private chats. Out of sight, out of mind, perhaps?

As I dove head first into my first full cyclocross season in two-decades, I was fully prepared for the problems to begin. Knowing that cross fans can be a toxic mixture of alcohol and bravado, I fully expected there to be issues, and perhaps I was wound too tight, waiting for those punches to land.

Before the season even started, a well-known bike industry personality tried to get into an argument with me and my friends over the fairness of me racing. At the first race of the season, I was dead named by master's guy I had known years prior. It was probably innocent on his part, but it caused me to fall apart.

A few weeks later, I was heckled at a race when a spectator shouted, "Get on his wheel!" to the woman behind me as we battled it out for midpack Cat three glory. Then, later in the season, I got into a shouting match with a spectator who persisted in yelling "man" and "dude" at me during a race.

Then, yet again, at Cross Nationals in Reno I was taunted by a spectator to zip up my jersey, as the sight of my sports bra and meager breasts must have been funny or offensive to him. I took to social media to complain about it because, "fuck you, I was hot!"

How is it that I found acceptance and a sense of community within cycling through being heckled? The common thread of each of these incidents are that they were provoked by cis-white men flexing their privilege and instinctive nature to harass women. But also, in each case the first people to jump to my defense and shout back with me were other women. As with many things in the trans experience, because I am forced to be skeptical and ask myself, "Am I accepted by the other women as an equal or is there just a shared experience in being on the receiving end of abuse from men?" I didn't have an answer to this then, and all of these months later, I still don't yet have one.

As I soft pedaled along a suburban Connecticut road early last week, a car rolled up next to me. The driver yelled "fucking faggot" and drove away. This taunt that I had heard countless times as a male cyclist now dysphorically stung. I simply would have preferred to have been heckled like every other woman who rides.

BOTH/AND

Jason

cw: *abuse, bullying, intersexism, car crash, injury*

I'm different. I always have been. When I was born, I was supposed to have a twin, but, due to complications in utero, I absorbed my twin. The absorption caused a chromosomal mutation in me, and I was born intersex. Largely because of this, I identify as agender. Due to the complications surrounding my birth, my parents chose to frame my existence as being a murderer of my unborn sibling and I was targeted for abuse by the people who were supposed to raise, love, and nurture me.

I had older siblings who were shown love and who were accepted for who they were, because they fit into our parents' preconceived notions of how people should look and behave. Anything outside of a strict gender binary was ridiculed. It wasn't just my family—there was no escaping the biases, fears, and hatred of people in the small town where I grew up. Kids at school simply regurgitated what they were told at home, and I was a victim of bullying everywhere I went. In various parts of my life, ignorance has escalated to physical violence against me. Just as the feeling of otherness has been common throughout my life, so have two other things—pain and bicycles.

When I was sixteen, I was involved in a severe and horrifying car crash. I was hit by someone running a stop sign and plowing into the driver-side of my car. I broke multiple bones, including my back, hip, and knee and was left requiring the use of a wheelchair for over a year and a half. During that time of being completely dependent and invisible, I slowly began to believe what others were saying around me—I was a freak for the way I looked, a freak for the way my body worked, I should have never been born, I was a mistake. I didn't know if I would ever walk again or if there was any point in trying. I certainly have no idea what convinced me to get on a bike at that time, but to say it saved my life is a gross understatement. Not only did bikes allow me to walk again, they allowed me to better control my constant/chronic pain by having easy and regular aerobic exercise. They also allowed me a mental escape from all of the negativity around me. My love of bicycles was cemented.

I had always hoped that maybe my love of bicycles would lead me to meet others who shared my passion. I tried to find cycling clubs but was overwhelmed by the toxic masculinity, elitism, and misogyny I found there. How could these people claim to love bicycling as much as I do and not be accepting of fellow bike lovers? I never felt comfortable or safe in any bicycling group and never sought them out again but my desire to be involved persisted. I had hoped the environment would be different in bike shops but if anything it was even worse. Even though I have one of the strongest passions for bicycling and bike repair and have numerous hours of experience and technical training it's never enough. Anyone who doesn't present as male always has to work harder to prove their worth to the other mechanics and to the cyclists. I have not, cannot, and possibly never will feel safe enough in the bicycling community to be 'out' about my identity unless there is a drastic cultural change.

The gender gap ratio in cyclists is three men for every woman. That gap is far larger in bike shops. It's extremely volatile to be working in such a hostile environment where anyone who isn't heterosexual and/or male is seen as less informed or less skilled in cycling and repair. Of all the places that 'mansplaining' is prevalent, none more so than in bike shops, which only further discourages women and nonbinary people from getting the products and services they need to enjoy bicycling. This is why it's important for everyone involved in cycling to be aware of this gap and to be aware that women, trans, and non-binary folk can *not* feel safe in the bicycling community.

But it's not just about awareness, it's about making small cultural changes that make a huge difference. If you see something unacceptable—speak up. When you meet someone new you don't know anything, let alone everything, about them so treat them with dignity and respect. It's these little actions that can make all the difference in making our community a safer and more inclusive space. Women, trans, non-binary, and intersex folk *can* help make a difference and lead new generations in and out of the bike shop and on and off of the bike. Together we can be the change we want to see and inspire others.

EXCERPTS FROM AND ADDITIONS TO *THE CASE FOR SLOW SPORT*

Eli Sachse

So much of sport culture is about discouraging. Society ends up discouraging us directly and indirectly, intentionally and unintentionally. Society thinks it means well; it thinks it protects us from harm and shame, but in reality, it is the very thing that causes shame.

We may not think of the things that society says to us as discouraging. But think about it. People seem to instinctively ask how much time your hike, run or ride took.

But what are they really asking when they ask that?

They are asking you to compare your performance to some societal standard. Why?

Sometimes people ask because they think they are being encouraging and engaged. Sometimes, they will follow with "Wow, that's great! I could never do something that hard." This self-denigration is also instinctual, ingrained by society. So there is discouragement going both ways. This is how we have been trained to think.

Why do we ask the questions we do? Why do we think that faster is better? Or longer?

Start slow. You'll get it. You'll get there.

When I was a kid, I had no role models or encouragement in cycling, backpacking or running. I was only told about how dangerous these things must be, by people who have never done any of them. I was told that I probably wasn't strong enough to carry everything I needed, that I ought to get a big, strong man to carry things for me and lead me. This didn't feel right. These endurance sports called to me because of the apparent challenge of knowing just how much one really can carry, for how long, and what one must need. Logistics. I didn't want someone to solve the logistics problems for me. That seemed to defeat the purpose. I wanted the elegance of independence in the wilderness.

Cook outside. Cook on a wood fire.

You will come across people who will try to make you feel less-than because they think their goals are loftier than yours. Just tell them, "Thats nice." "Good for you." Talking to big, strong people in a subtly diminutive fashion is so very rewarding and just on so many levels.

Their goal might be to go longer and faster. But your goals are to enjoy life, get strong, see amazing things, and share the beauty of nature with everyone. Your goals are better.

Try and fail a few times, and you will quickly amass a body of knowledge about the sport that surpasses these kinds of detractors. And if you want to, and work at it, someday you'll go faster than them.

People who are truly skilled and confident in their sport encourage others. People who discourage are ignorant.

Make time to play in the water.

If you're small, there will be people who walk faster than you. It doesn't mean they are more fit. It means they have longer legs. The same hike might take you longer. This doesn't mean you are weaker.

Stop to take pictures. People who rush through beautiful places are morons.

Cis-het normies like to think they own the wilderness because they think they are fit and beautiful and the world revolves around them and their selfies. They are super duper wrong. The wilderness belongs to everyone, especially confident queer folks.

Although, if you are discouraged by the crowds in national parks, you can also try going in winter. It is sublime.

Also, the USA is spoiled with vast areas of wilderness. There are oftentimes plenty of amazing campsites and trails just adjacent to National Parks, that have a fraction of the traffic.

Camp on BLM land (Bureau of Land Management). It's free for everyone.

Queers are taking over nature, and y'all better watch out.

I SWEAR YOU NEVER LANDED AGAIN

Connor Rose Delisle

cw: alcohol, death

I don't remember the first time I really rode a bike. What I do remember is looking at GT Bicycle catalogs in a kid's clubhouse, about fifteen years years ago. Dave Mirra had just landed the first double backflip and flatland was still a thing. Mirra **also** wasn't dead yet. Neither was my friend.

My first real bike was a BMX, a Haro Revo Mag. We built ramps out of old plywood and cinder blocks and jumped farther and higher every year. I didn't learn any tricks. We just pushed the landing ramp farther and farther back until the speed and the distance became too terrifying to attempt. In high school we outgrew our front yards and rode out across the highway and past the county line. I built a better bike this time, collecting parts at every holiday: a brake for Christmas, new cranks on my birthday. Eventually these bits—a growing stack of Dan's Comp boxes—were enough to build a weapon against something I hadn't named yet. I rode more, not to get better but to never stop riding. Time was traded for abrasions and photographs in an endless urgent push to never stop and never take account.

Jamie was the kid with the clubhouse. He was the first one to have the nicest bike and the best life. He grew up, and stopped riding bikes, and went to school, and moved on. He built a life. He did not drink to excess, never came out as gay or queer or trans, never went to jail, and did not die young. He was a good person and as far as I know still is one.

Bobby is my friend who's dead. We rode bikes together from before I can remember, looking at the GT catalog in a clubhouse, until he grew older and bored and moved on. He started drinking and kept going. He took a long pause and then he was gone. In my favorite picture I have of him, he's standing on his homemade ramp, about to fall down.

Somewhere in between all that, life and not, I changed, too. I let my BMX bike go flat in my parent's garage, and I became a fixie kid in the late aughts. I took someone else's old piece of shit and made it my own piece of shit. I rode around New York City and North Carolina with one crappy front brake and broken spokes and no helmet and not a goddamn clue. I was smiling and terrified and alone.

Bikes have always meant possibility to me. "My bike takes me places that school never could." To watch something like Stephen Hamilton's part in the Animal *Can I Eat?* video is to watch the world transformed. It is not mystical but it is threateningly sublime. I'm a terrible dancer, but I can move on a bike and feel smooth and lucid and free.

I like to drink and I drank too much, but many people do. I rode my bike and never stopped and rode headlong into disaster after disaster feeling more terrible every year. I came out as trans in my basement apartment in Midwood in a jumble of carpet and faux wood paneling in the summer of 2012. Every estrangement I ever felt from my own soft and fleshy body stretched out before me and snapped into place like a tentpole propping up my life. Riding and building and fixing bikes gave me something to focus on that wasn't *me*, at least not in the here and now. Bikes gave me a thread that ran through my life, one that could stitch the past to the present in a way that was textured, coherent, and un-gendered. That history of beautiful machines defined who I had been, and meant to be, with more honesty than anything else I could grab hold of. When I ride now I am ten years old and sixteen and 26 all at once, holding in me everyone who has shared in that story, even if their chapter has ended.

When I ride a bike, my embodiment becomes irrelevant. I am balance and velocity and nothing else. I am alert and lucid and sober. I am alive and standing.

I WISH I LIKED ANYTHING AS MUCH AS I LOVE MY BIKE, OR: HOW FIXING MY BIKE TAUGHT ME TO HATE MYSELF LESS

Hannah Burt

cw: self-harm, suicidal ideation, disordered eating

I buy my bike on October 24th. It's been 36 days since, sitting at my laptop in a crowded coffee shop, I admit to myself for the first time that I am not a girl. I am not quite a boy either—I do not yet have the words to describe my experience. It's a red 70s Shogun road bike I find on Craigslist—steel frame, heavy steel wheels. $100. I know almost nothing about bikes but I know that I love this particular bike as soon as I take the handlebars and swing my leg over the seat. My bike does not have a name for a long time. I want to wait until something feels right. She is an old bike with a mysterious past but, as I discover, a fierce sense of loyalty. I do not have a name for my genderless body for a long time either. Eventually it comes to me. I name her Evelyn.

I do not know how to take care of my bike for a long time. I leave her outside. It rains. It snows. I ride every day that first New England winter and, although I do not take care of my bike, she does not fail me.

I do not know how to take care of my trans body either. I used to think that everyone hated their body the way that I did, that it was just a part of growing up. But finding a label for my experience—as trans, as non-binary—does not lead to the healing and easy self-acceptance that I had hoped. Reliving my life through this new lens, I only feel my anxiety and resentment more intensely. I spent years burying an identity I did not have the words for and the excavation process will be painful and slow. I do not know how to heal my past. I do not know how to exist in the present. How can my non-binary body survive in a binary world?

I fall back on old habits I thought I had left behind me. I restrict my food, hoping that the soft parts of me will disappear. I steal my roommate's pocket knife and draw angry red lines on my calves and thighs. I resent my hips, my slim hands, my soft voice--any of the tells that betray the fragile androgyny I am trying to build into armor.

I dream that I am a boy. I dream that I am dead. I don't know which I want more. My shoulders hold constant tension.

I keep biking. Feet on pedals, legs moving rhythmically, it is the only time my body feels like it was built for something good. Like I am able to move forward.

I shave my head. I change my pronouns on social media. I tell one friend to call me 'they', then one more. I wonder if I will ever have the nerve to tell my parents. I start binding my chest.

I manage to get hired as a bike mechanic that spring, and I spend my first season caring for other people's bikes better than I ever cared for mine. At the shop, my anxious shoulders give way to aching muscles from wrestling off half-seized cranksets and hauling heavy bikes up and down the stairs. I grow stronger and in small moments, with my dirty hands navigating the bike in front of me, I feel useful. Like my body is capable of fixing something that has been broken.

I start bringing my bike inside at night. She is in rough shape. I have not looked at the damage the hard riding and long winters have done to her. I have avoided acknowledging what she needs, because I am ashamed at how bad I have let things get. I don't look at my bike when I ride. I don't look at my body either if I can help it. Eventually, after more than a year of neglect, I feel her brakes starting to give out. She is asking for help. Help is something I do not know how to ask for myself yet, but I know I can start by helping her.

I bring her into the shop one evening after work and lift her into a stand. It is a long process to rebuild something nearly lost. It takes ten minutes just to wrest the seatpost from her frame. But I do it. We fall into a rhythm. Staying late after work, turning the music up, we start healing each other. I take my time cleaning, re-greasing, and lubricating each part. I replace the brakes. Install a new chain and freewheel. Replace old cablesets and resurrect the front derailleur, nearly mummified with years of grime.

I build my first wheels. Instruction manual in hand, I drop spokes into the hub one at a time, slowly lacing each into the rim. At the truing stand I add tension slowly, bringing the wheel into round. The methodical approach is a new feeling to me. I feel a connection to body as my hands flex each set of spokes. I realize how unfamiliar this tenderness feels. I do not remember the last time I treated my own body so carefully.

I start putting simple tasks on my daily to-do list. Eat dinner. Take a shower. Go outside. Survive.

Healing is never a job that is finished. Neither is bike repair. There will always be brake pads that wear out or a hub in need of adjustment. I have bad days still and when I do, I grab my bike and head for the nearest path that will leave the crowded city behind me. My feet on the pedals, trees on either side of us, I breathe. My body is meant for this. My bike does not care about the width of my hips and the shape of my chest. Propelled as one, I feel that on my bike, my body can be something I do not have to resent.

Do not be fooled; this is not a happy ending. My happy ending can not exist in a binary world. But for now, I am eating regularly. I return my roommate's pocket knife. I am trying to treat myself with the same kindness which with I have learned to treat my bike. I am starting to accept that I may never feel at home in this body of mine, but I am working on it. And until then, I have my bike.

PUTTING THE TRANS BACK IN TRANSPORTATION

René Rivera

cw: internalized transphobia

In June of last year, 2017, I came out as transgender to somewhere between ten and twenty thousand people. I would have done almost anything to avoid this, but as the executive director of a dynamic and fast-growing bicycle advocacy organization, there was just no way to avoid making my coming out process very, very public.

I was born female-bodied and, on the inside, male-identified. Growing up I didn't hear about trans folks until I was in my late twenties. Even in the Bay Area, there wasn't much trans visibility in the 70s and 80s when I was a kid and teenager. Once I did meet other trans folk in the 90s I knew that is what I was, but was also deeply committed to a butch lesbian feminist identity and it felt to me that I would be betraying everything I believed in to jump ship and become a man. Transitioning felt like it would be abandoning everything I knew and loved to join an enemy camp. It has taken me many years to understand that I can take on the healing of toxic masculinity within my own mind and body and that transitioning to male does not mean abandoning my commitment to feminism, my belief in the power of the feminine or my own work to honor and lift up the female within me and in our culture and communities.

I have never fit in as a bicycle advocacy leader. I got started in this movement twenty years ago volunteering for the San Francisco Bicycle Coalition, a good place to start. There were lots of other queer folks involved at all levels and women were key leaders in the organization. In my Bay Area bubble, I didn't know, until I took my current position as executive director (ED) of Bike East Bay, that bicycle advocacy in the rest of the country was a very white cis- and straight male space.

I remember the first national meeting of bicycle advocacy leaders I went to after starting my role as ED six years ago.

Arriving at the Thunderhead Ranch in Wyoming for a gathering of 40 or so EDs of bicycle advocacy groups across the country, I was shocked to find that 80% or so of the group was was straight white cis-dudes, and most of those with beards. As a mixed race, gender non-conforming butch dyke, I definitely did not see myself reflected in this group of leaders at all. As I have joked many times since, the one thing I had in common with the majority of the group was that I also have a beard.

Over the years as a bicycle advocacy leader I have kept close track of how many other leaders fall into any category other than straight, white and cis-male. Women? More and more all the time. People of color? Between zero and one at any given time. Queer? A few, mostly white and cis-male. Trans or gender-nonconforming? Zero, until Tamika Butler joined the Los Angeles County Bicycle Coalition as executive director in 2014.

Tamika's hire was like a life buoy thrown into the mostly white male cisgender leadership pool of bicycle advocacy. Within hours of getting this news that a black, gender-nonconforming lesbian executive director had joined the pool I sent off an email to Tamika to say "Hey, I am here, I've got your back and will support you however I can."

Three years later Tamika has left the LACBC. I hope that the world of bicycle advocacy will never be the same. She called bullshit on the movement with kindness and humor at every panel and keynote she was invited to. She held up the mirror to the movement to show the homogeneity, and yes, often racism, that is deep in our movement.

For me personally, Tamika kept me going, helped me feel less alone in my role, and showed me that there is space in this movement to be totally, authentically myself. It is very hard to be a leader in a space where you do not see yourself reflected back. To have even one person reflect me was life-saving.

What kind of leadership does this movement need right now? If we are going to reach beyond the white wonky bro culture of transportation geeks talking to other transportation geeks we need leaders that embody other experiences. We need leaders who have a lived experience of racism, oppression, trauma, and poverty. We need leaders who know how to listen, empathize, partner, put themselves in other's shoes, and tell the difficult truths.

We also need to recognize that these unlikely leaders are doing the work of shifting our culture for all of us, and we need to support them. We are not going to get beyond one or two POC executive directors, a handful of women, a few queer and trans folks, unless we recognize that it is everyone's responsibility to shift the culture of our movement, not the responsibility of those few who are so uncomfortable and obviously outside the norm that they have to do the work just to survive. And of course they burn out and leave before too long.

As I came to the point in my own journey where I knew I needed to live in the world as a man, the prospect of coming out in my role as executive director was my biggest fear. In my community I was already trans identified. My family knows me so well, there would be no surprise and only support there. It was the prospect of entering totally uncharted territory that terrified me. I could not find another executive director, or leader of a public-facing organization of any kind, who had come out as trans on the job. While there are growing numbers of trans folk who hold elected office and other leadership positions, there are few who have gone through their transitions in a public role. Many take advantage of job transitions to change their name and pronouns.

For months, though I knew it was my heart's desire to transition, I was completely stopped by being unable to imagine what this process would be like, coming out as a leader and the face of a well-known organization. Finally I had to just take the leap and have faith I would figure out how to fly on the way down.

I had been working on taking a two month mini-sabbatical from my job, and in many ways this was the catalyst for me to take this leap. It took a year and a half to put all the plans in place for me to be able to step away from my job for those two months. As this time came closer it became clear to me that this was the best chance I would have to give myself the time and space to make this momentous change.

Before leaving, I shared with my staff team that I was transitioning and that most likely when I returned, I would be asking them to use different pronouns. They were enthusiastically supportive, as I knew they would be.

Figuring out how to tell my board was much harder. Normally, if you are taking the steps to transition at work you would go to your boss or to the human resources director and they would support you in the process and manage all communications with others in the organization. As ED, I was both the boss and the human resources person. There was no-one to support me.

I chose one board member who I trusted and who was already well educated in trans and gender issues to be my champion and advocate with the board. There was no way I was going to get up at a board meeting and tell fifteen board members about my transition! Talking to fifteen people individually also felt impossible! My board member champion took on communicating with my board on my behalf while I was away.

In retrospect, my time off was incredibly supportive to me at this time because I had the time to sit with my own decision and to come back 100% sure of what I was doing. It also helped my organization because the staff and board had those two months to get used to this change, to educate themselves on trans and gender issues, to practice using new pronouns, and to support each other around any fears that came up for them in having their leader make such a big life change.

I returned to an organization that was behind me and my decision to transition and to come out as transgender to our broader community. Even with such amazing support it still felt to me like stepping off a cliff to enter into this public phase of my professional coming out process. I still couldn't imagine it, even as I knew that I had to do it and that there was no going back.

Ultimately, I tackled my own coming out process as I would any other task or campaign, I put a spreadsheet together with every step in the process, every person and group I needed to contact, and how I would contact them and in what sequence. Then I worked my way through the plan.

This started with reaching out directly to key partners and donors to tell them I am transgender and ask them to use masculine pronouns. A month or two later, it culminated with sharing a letter in our e-newsletter and print newsletter and finally coming out on social media. In this final public push to all our members and supporters I estimate the news went to somewhere between ten and twenty thousand people. Of course, not all of them clicked through or read my letter, but nonetheless it was out there.

To my surprise, it was really at this point that the weight of what I was doing really slammed down on me. It was easier when the coming out process was a plan to execute against. Once it was done I had the most massive vulnerability hangover imaginable. I think I imagined that doing what felt impossible would be a massive relief, or would be celebratory. Instead it triggered deep, survival level fear. I had done that thing that I was never supposed to do—I had put myself first and asked the world to adapt to my needs. In some deep part of my unconscious it felt like I would lose everything for having done this, for having so completely broken the rules.

I was struggling to understand why, at the end of this coming out process, I felt like crawling into a cave and never coming out. I was talking with one of my mentors and he totally got it. He said, you are pushing the culture to change, you are doing the deep and enormous work of change for the culture. I imagined myself pushing a giant rock up a mountain, and yes, it felt like that.

I know that a year from now, or five or ten years from now this will all feel very different. But it is good to stop right here and reflect on this. To really see the work it has taken to show up authentically in my leadership role, the personal cost and the personal benefit.

I also recognize that I am very lucky to be in the Bay Area where I am so supported. It can feel almost surreal to be coming out so publicly with no push back, when I know other trans folk are being discriminated against and killed across our country. I am privileged. At the same time, the news warns me and tells me every day, "your life is worthless, you are less than human." To be at a time like this where so much is changing is incredibly complicated.

There have been points where the cost has felt too great. At those times, what gets me through is the hope that I am walking a path that others can follow, that I am making a map through the impossible. I hope that another leader faced with an impossible choice will be able to say, well René did it, maybe I can too.

I believe deeply that we need new leaders right now. I think it's clear to all of us that majority leadership by privileged straight white cisgender men is not working for us. I am dedicated to creating space for and lifting up the rest of us to leadership. I think it is the only hope we have to save our world. Lucky for me I work in a movement that reflects the dominant culture. If we can change the bicycle advocacy movement and bring in leaders of color, more women, queer and trans leaders, and leaders who have experienced poverty and trauma, then we can change the rest of the world too.

"KEEP the FAITH"

ABOUT THE CONTRIBUTORS

Connor Rose is a trans femme cyclist living and riding in LA. They enjoy petting cats, battling the heteropatriarchy, and cooking pasta with their partner, Emily.

Eli Sachse is a photographer, painter, and writer. He finds his inspiration in cycling, backpacking, cross country skiing, rock climbing, and being super queer and trans. Find his books at Microcosm Publishing and Blurb.com.

Elly Bangs was raised in a new age cult, had six wisdom teeth, and likes to ride her bike a long long way. She lives by the Salish Sea, fixing machines by day and writing under cover of darkness. Her short stories have appeared in *Daily Science Fiction*, *Strange Horizons*, and *Bikes In Space*—and her dystopian novels will be coming out one of these days, she swears. Learn more about her and read her work at elbangs.com / @elly_bangs.

Hannah Burt is a Midwest-raised, non-binary bike mechanic living in New England. If they aren't on their bike, you can find them knitting, cooking, or dreaming up new ways to topple the patriarchy.

Jace is a pansy transsexual bicycle mechanic in Boston. You can find them in the shop, on the trails, or sometimes on the internet at @uhh_jace.

Jason is a 26 year old intersex individual who identifies as agender who loves to bicycle. They live with DID, other disabilities both physical and neurological, and chronic pain. They are a strong advocate for all minorities, focusing hardest on LGBT, Intersex folk, and those living with disabilities for more inclusion and safety in spaces.

Laurie Williams is a UK-based filmmaker and regular volunteer at London Bike Kitchen, a do-it-together bike workshop. When they're not filming or cycling, they like boxing, catsitting and listening to podcasts in the bath.

Liz Tetu (sometimes Ulysses) is a white bi guy who writes comics and essays about sex, digital media, and himself. His pieces show up in zines like *Cartoon Punk: Artists Against Fascism* and the *Queer-Spirit Charity Zine*. He's twenty and kind of funny.

Lydia Rogue is a writer and poet living in Portland, Oregon. They write about the environment and queer issues, when they're not writing sappy love poems for their girlfriend. You can find them online at lydiarogue.com.

Quinn is a trans woman bike mechanic. She lives in Michigan with her girlfriends and their three dogs.

René Rivera is a leader and bridge-builder, working and learning in all the spaces in-between race, gender, and other perceived binaries, as a trans, queer, mixed-race maverick bike dork. He has led bicycle advocacy groups for the last eight years as acting executive director of the San Francisco Bicycle Coalition in 2010 and as executive director of Bike East Bay since then. He is also a long-time meditator and serves as board member and diversity chair at Spirit Rock Meditation Center.

Rufus Isabel Elliot (https://www.ambf.co.uk/music) is an agender composer and musician, interested in the interactions of wildness, queerness, musicality and listening. Rufus has written funerary marches for spaceships, and orchestral music about rotting seaweed, which have been performed in venues such as the Tate Modern and Bold Tendencies (London). It is currently studying for its MMus in Composition at the Royal Conservatoire of Scotland.

Sybil Collas is a narrative designer, for video games and other things, and a writer. They have a passion for universes of fiction and will stop at nothing to champion their vision of a world where representation is part of the norm—steadily creating LGBTQ+ characters defined not only by their queer identity, but by their dreams, fears, and values. Check out their website: ineedastory.com.

Tara Seplavy is a 42-year old cyclist who resides in New York and Connecticut. She is a mother of two, a Cat three road and cyclocross racer, a mountain biker for over 25-years, and has worked in the bicycle industry for over twenty years. She is currently the Director of Brand Advocacy for GT Bicycles. She can be found being snarky about bike racing, the bike industry, and sometimes music on Twitter & Instagram at @t_seplavy.

Trista Vercher is a queer, trans artist currently working in Portland, OR. They like to make art that explores the themes of gender and mental health to challenge stereotypes and encourage self-empowerment through sharing stories. Mostly though, they just draw their cats or read while cuddling with said cats. www.vercherink.com/about

LIFELINE

877-565-8860

HOTLINES

One day, I dream we won't live in a world where I feel like leaving out these numbers is irresponsible. I *want* to live in a world where we don't feel the need to list the Trans Lifeline on the cover of a zine like this.

However, the truth is that almost 50 percent of trans and nonbinary people have attempted suicide at some point in their lives. Here are some support lines and chats, because I know it can be hard sometimes. But here's the whole truth: the world wants you to still be here. *I* want you to still be here.

Many of these are volunteer run and/or non-profit. Consider donating or volunteering if you have the time, money, and/or energy to do so.

U.S. AND CANADA:

National Suicide Prevention Hotline:

For anyone and everyone in the US.

1-800-273-8255

SuicidePreventionLifeline.org

Trans Lifeline:

Specifically for trans and nonbinary individuals, this number is listed on the front of our zine.

1 (877) 565-8860 (USA)

1 (877) 330-6366 (Canada)

TransLifeLine.org

GLBT Hotline:

For anyone and everyone in the community.

1-888-843-4564

GLBTHotline.org

Trevor Project:

The Trevor Project is specifically for LGBT youth and is one of the most well-known charities helping people.

1 (866) 488-7386

TheTrevorProject.org

Sage:

For the older members of our community—while so often the focus is on our youth, you need support too.

1-888-234-SAGE (7243)

GLBTHotline.org/sage-hotline.html

UNITED KINGDOM:

London Lesbian & Gay Switchboard

020 7837 7324 (UK)

www.llgs.org.uk

Brighton & Hove LGBT Switchboard

01273 204050 (UK)

https://www.switchboard.org.uk

FRANCE:

English:

SOS Helpline

01 46 21 46 46—not available 24/7

http://www.soshelpline.org

French:

Fil Sante Jeunes—for young people aged 12-25

0800 235 236—not available 24/7

https://www.filsantejeunes.com—also has an online chat

SOS Amitie

09 72 39 40 50

https://www.sos-amitie.com— also has an online chat

OTHER AREAS:

These aren't necessarily LGBT specific, but there are hotlines all over the world so if you need help, there are many listed here.

en.wikipedia.org/wiki/List_of_suicide_crisis_lines

ONLINE CHAT:.

I hate talking on the phone, but that doesn't mean there isn't help if you're in the same boat as me.

The Trevor Project

TheTrevorProject.org/get-help-now—not available 24/7

GLBT Hotline

GLBTHotline.org/chat.html—not available 24/7

Building The Feminist

Bicycle Revolution Since 1996

Microcosm.Pub

Read more about the Bicycling Revolution:

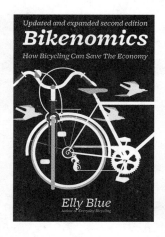

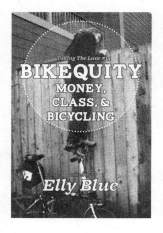

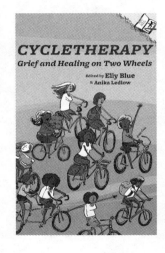

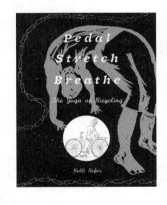

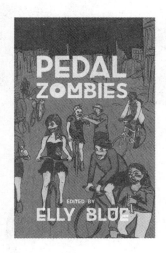

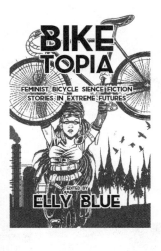

SUBSCRIBE TO EVERYTHING WE PUBLISH!

Do you love what Microcosm publishes?

Do you want us to publish more great stuff?

Would you like to receive each new title as it's published?

Subscribe as a BFF to our new titles and we'll mail them all to you as they are released!

$10-30/mo, pay what you can afford. Include your t-shirt size and your birthday for a possible surprise!

microcosmpublishing.com/bff